20 SIMPLE SHORTCUTS TO SMALL BUSINESS SUCCESS

KELLY EXETER

Copyright © 2016 by Kelly Exeter

All rights reserved.

Published in Australia by Swish Publishing, Perth, Western Australia.

www.swishpublishing.com.au

National Library of Australia Cataloguing-in-Publication entry

Author: Exeter, Kelly M., 1977- author.

Title: 20 Simple Shortcuts to Small Business Success/ Kelly Exeter.

ISBN: 978-0-9924416-5-4 (paperback)

Printed in the United States of America

First Edition

Cover Design, Book Design & Layout: Swish Design

Author photo: Angelique Lee

*For Anthony—everything I talk about in here
is stuff you told me years and years ago.
But still, I chose to learn the hard way. Here's hoping
readers of this book are smarter than me!*

CONTENTS

INTRODUCTION 1

SECTION 1: HEALTH 7

    Shortcut 1: Eight great nutrition tips for a
maximum energy day 9

    Shortcut 2: Stop sacrificing sleep 15

    Shortcut 3: Manage stress better
(be the egg, not the potato) 19

SECTION 2: NUMBERS 25

    Shortcut 4: You attract what you track 27

    Shortcut 5: Invoice smarter for better cash flow 31

    Shortcut 6: Make it super-easy for people
to buy from you 37

SECTION 3: PRODUCTIVITY 39

    Shortcut 7: Get up earlier (as opposed to 'early') 41

    Shortcut 8: Practise strategic procrastination 45

Shortcut 9: Stop starting again and eat the frog first. . . . 49

Shortcut 10: Re-think meetings. 53

Shortcut 11: Embrace routine. 57

Shortcut 12: Practise the one-minute rule 65

SECTION 4: MARKETING **67**

Shortcut 13: Leverage the power of storytelling 69

Shortcut 14: Market your business in 10 minutes a day . . 73

Shortcut 15: Get people to crave you 77

SECTION 5: MINDSET **81**

Shortcut 16: Stop saving, start investing—in yourself 83

Shortcut 17: Put yourself out there—
learn the art of asking 87

Shortcut 18: Be willing to narrow your focus 95

Shortcut 19: Set yourself up to make better decisions . . . 99

Shortcut 20: Get comfortable being uncomfortable. . . . 103

WHERE TO FROM HERE? **105**

ACKNOWLEDGEMENTS **107**

20 SIMPLE SHORTCUTS TO SMALL BUSINESS SUCCESS

KELLY EXETER

INTRODUCTION

Business success.

For many people today, those two words tend to conjure up an image of someone lying in a hammock on a tropical island, cocktail in hand, with their phone and laptop casually arranged on a side table next to them.

I'm pretty sure we can all blame Tim Ferris for that.

Thankfully, when I first started my web and graphic design business ten years ago, I hadn't come across *The 4-Hour Workweek* yet.

At that point in time, I defined 'business success' as being able to make as much from my business as I'd been making in the day job I'd just left. And, thanks to the network of contacts I'd built up before going out on my own, I quickly achieved that level of business success.

So my definition then shifted. It became being able to take a holiday without experiencing a massive downturn in income while I was away. That too was achieved fairly quickly, this time by bringing on a staff member.

Then I got pregnant, and my definition of business success changed yet again. Now the business needed to be able to operate without me in the office for an extended period. This was achieved—but only barely. I'd set the business up to *survive* without me in it, but not *thrive*.

Eighteen months later, when I had a complete breakdown from the combined stresses of running a rapidly growing business while also managing a household and being the mother of a newborn, business success was the last thing on my mind.

I didn't even want to have a business anymore. It all just seemed too hard.

Fortunately for me, my husband was available to step in and take on the role of General Manager in what was now 'our' business.

(That one action showed me that business success for creative people can mean handing over the minutiae of running a business so you can get back to doing what you love: being creative.)

In the years since 'my business' became 'our business,' our definition of business success has continued to evolve from:

- Me being able to stay away from the business for three months when our second child was born (achieved), to
- Me being able to greatly reduce my role in our business once our first child started school (achieved), to
- The business being able to survive a major, *major* business disaster (achieved), to

- The business being able to survive a major, *major* downturn in the economy (achieved).

However, there's one definition of business success we've not yet been able to achieve—my long-held dream of running a business that never faces any challenges. It's only taken ten years, but I've finally realised that dream is a bit silly.

In the same way that growth in life comes from surmounting challenges, so too does growth in business.

Take away the challenges, and you take away the potential for growth.

Which is why I have a new definition for business success these days.

It's one where both a business and its owners have the resilience needed to surmount all the challenges thrown their way.

Challenges like:

- Losing a major client
- Entry of a well-financed competitor into the market
- A product that was a major money maker suddenly becoming irrelevant
- Depressed economies
- Illness.

How does a business (and its owners) develop this resilience?

Experience gained the hard way over the past ten years has taught me these five things are key:

1. Prioritising health

When things get busy or hard in business, the first thing we tend to do is sacrifice sleep and exercise and fall into poor nutrition habits. This is the very definition of 'false economy.' Good health should be a focus and priority at all times, but it becomes even more important when we're under the pump in our businesses and need the energy to do good work, make good decisions, and be across everything we need to be across.

2. Knowing the numbers

You can't manage what you don't measure. Once you start paying attention to things like sales figures, profit margins and email subscribers, something magical happens—it becomes very clear where money and time is being wasted. This allows you to tighten up systems and processes and get rid of services (and even clients) that are trashing your bottom line. Suddenly you have a business that is more profitable, has better cash flow and causes you a lot less stress!

3. Increasing productivity

It feels like we all have so much to do and such little time to do it. And it's very easy to get caught up doing stuff that feels like it's setting us up for business success, but is really just 'busy-work'. So the first rule of productivity is getting your priorities right—

ensuring the tasks you are working on are actually taking you closer to your business and life goals. The second is ensuring you have the energy to tackle those tasks with vigour. The third involves managing your time properly to ensure the truly important stuff gets done.

4. Ongoing marketing

If there is one mistake I see consistently across all small business owners it's this: they only start marketing their business when work suddenly and unexpectedly dries up. The problem with this is, the best form of marketing is the kind that builds genuine relationships. And that form of marketing needs to be ongoing over years, not weeks. If you only ever market your business from a place of scarcity, everything becomes tinged with desperation. I don't think I need to tell you how off-putting this is to the people on the receiving end of it!

5. Developing a resilient mindset

Running a business is hard, there's just no getting around that fact. As I've already pointed out, however, it's good that it's hard. It's good that it throws challenges our way, because great personal and professional growth comes out of those challenges. The key to taking on those challenges is having a mindset that is willing to tackle them head-on rather than fall into victim mode and wonder 'Why do these things keep happening to me?'. When you're growing a business, a strong mind is unquestionably your biggest asset.

Shortcuts to business success

"There's no elevator to success; you have to take the stairs."

We've all heard that, right?

Well, I respectfully disagree. Over the past ten years I've done everything the hard way and I can see many occasions where I could have fast-tracked my development by taking one simple shortcut: learning from other people's mistakes instead of having to make them all myself.

That's where this book comes in.

You know those five elements I mentioned above that are key to developing business resilience: health, numbers, productivity, marketing and mindset?

This book lays out 20 of the most useful things I've learned in those categories. My goal, as always, is to:

- Keep things as simple as possible
- Share only the things I know work (because they worked for me)
- Share things that anyone can action, right now.

You don't need an MBA or a marketing degree or any special skills to do the things on the following pages. You just need the drive and desire to make your small business a success.

SECTION 1: HEALTH

SHORTCUT 1:
EIGHT GREAT NUTRITION TIPS FOR A MAXIMUM ENERGY DAY

We can't change the number of hours we have in a day. But we can change the energy we bring to those hours. That's why I do my best to get a good dose of quality sleep (more on this in the next shortcut) and make sure I exercise every day.

But I've noticed there are days when I can tick both the sleep and exercise boxes and still be struggling to find the energy to concentrate and be productive—especially in the afternoon.

When this happens, it's usually because I've missed another crucial piece of the puzzle—good nutrition.

Of course, thanks to the media and the internet it's hard to even know what 'good nutrition' is these days. Is it eating Paleo? Ditching gluten? Fasting two days a week?

Forget all those things. Good nutrition for a maximum energy day is much easier to achieve than you might think. Here are my eight best tips:

1. Start your day with two big glasses of water

This might seem pretty random but it was part of a health challenge I once did, and it made such a difference to my life it's now a habit.

The first thing I do when I wake up in the morning is head to the kitchen and have two really large glasses of water. Rather than trying to knock them back in one minute, I spend 10-15 minutes scrolling through Instagram or Facebook while I drink. It's a chilled way to start the day, and those fluids seem to get my whole system going (in a good way).

And even if I forget to drink any more water for the rest of the day (which can happen), those two big glasses really seem to go the distance.

2. Have a green smoothie for breakfast

If there's one great thing you can do for both your health and your energy levels right now, it's to stop having cereal for breakfast. Every breakfast cereal on the market (other than rolled oats and Weet-Bix) is loaded with sugar. And chances are you add sugar to rolled oats and Weet-Bix for taste anyway.

The other problem with cereal is it's not designed to get you through to lunch. By 10:30am you're running out of energy, and need a snack/morning tea to keep you going. So much so, we all think needing a snack around 10:30am is 'normal'.

Enter the green smoothie. The beauty of these (when they're made well) is that they tick so many boxes. Even the most basic recipes provide plenty of fluids and 1-2 serves of vegetables. If you add good-quality protein powder and some healthy fats, you have a more 'complete' meal that can get you all the way to lunch. (Well, once you break the habit of heading to the biscuit jar at 10:30am every day.)

What do you put in a green smoothie?

Head to **swishdesign.com.au/green** for a helpful guide and free download.

3. Always take a lunch break

By this I mean 'get away from your desk at lunchtime'. While we all tend to eat lunch, too many of us eat it at our desks—one hand holding a sandwich while the other taps away on the keyboard.

That's not great for our energy levels later in the day.

It's really important to move away from your desk and try to eat your lunch in a mindful fashion. All you need is ten minutes to give your brain a rest and ensure it picks up on the fact you've actually eaten. Believe me, you'll get those ten minutes back many times over in the afternoon.

4. Don't buy your lunch from the lunch bar

I'm not saying there aren't any healthy options at that lunch bar. There probably are. But when you're faced with the choice between delicious hot chips and a healthy salad, the hot chips will generally win out. Then you'll spend so much time berating yourself for your lack of willpower over those chips that you'll struggle to get all your work done in the afternoon.

5. Understand that it's okay to feel hungry

The ready availability of food in the modern world means it's very easy for us to 'graze' our way through the day. Which means that if you're anything like me you'll head for the pantry or fridge at the first grumble of your stomach.

The problem is that the more food choices we have to make over the course of a day, the harder it is to make them all good ones. And another thing: if our stomachs spend all day processing food then guess what? We're going to feel sluggish and slow all day.

So learn to understand the difference between being peckish and being hungry. If you're eating three truly nourishing meals a day (more on that in a second), any tummy rumblings outside your regular meal times are most likely peckishness—something that can be quickly banished with a big glass of water.

6. Stop eating from packets

If you're eating something from a packet, there's a good chance it contains added sugar, preservatives and half a dozen ingredients you can't even pronounce.

None of these are good for your health. They adversely affect the way your body functions, and anything that does that will affect your energy levels too. So try and eat food you've made from scratch as much as possible.

And for those times when it isn't possible, stick to packet foods that:

- Have less than 5% sugar
- Don't contain preservatives
- Have a minimal number of ingredients
- Don't contain ingredients with numbers, or names you can't pronounce.

7. Embrace good fats

Ah, fat. The mortal enemy for as long as I've been alive. Thankfully, most of us have now caught on to the fact that it's not fat that's making us fat. It's our penchant for packaged and processed foods that are high in sugar and other weird things (such as those ingredients with numbers and names we can't pronounce).

So, why should you embrace good fats? Well, one of their many benefits is they make you feel fuller for longer and stop you running to the pantry every five minutes.

How do you get more good fats into your diet? Eat full-fat dairy (milk, cheese, yoghurt, butter) rather than the low-fat alternatives. Add half an avocado and/or a handful of nuts to your salads. Make your own salad dressings from olive, macadamia or avocado oil rather than using commercial dressings. And add a tablespoon of coconut oil to your green smoothie.

8. Time your caffeine hits for maximum effect

If you've been a coffee drinker for any length of time, it probably has very little impact on your energy levels and mental alertness (unless you're particularly sensitive to caffeine). But with the right timing, even the most habitual coffee drinkers can get a caffeine boost.

How do you time your caffeine hit right? By having it when your cortisol levels are at their lowest. So, rather than having a coffee first thing in the morning when your cortisol levels are naturally high, time it for mid-morning and mid-afternoon when they've taken a dip.

But limit yourself to just coffee or tea. Having a sugar-filled biscuit as well will cancel out the energy boosting effect of your well-timed coffee break.

SHORTCUT 2: STOP SACRIFICING SLEEP

Sleep. It's the first thing that gets sacrificed when life gets busy. And there's no busier life than that of the average business owner.

We're never on top of our workloads, and we never reach the end of our to-do lists. So we start staying up a little later, getting up a little earlier, and kidding ourselves that we can function perfectly well on four or five hours sleep a night.

And technically, we can. But there's a big difference between functioning and thriving. And thriving is where we need to be. If you start every day feeling tired, it won't be long before your business starts looking pretty tired as well.

So what can we do to:

1. Get better quality sleep?

2. Get more sleep than we're currently getting?

I have these ten tips to offer:

1. Your last job each day should be to schedule out the next day

When you know exactly what the next day holds you won't waste vital mental energy trying to remember what you need to do tomorrow, or spend time wondering what's in store for the next day. This helps reduce anxiety (which can be a big sleep smasher).

2. No coffee after 3pm, and no alcohol less than two hours before bedtime

Caffeine and alcohol affect our ability to both fall asleep and sleep deeply. Following these recommendations means you can enjoy them and still get a good night's sleep.

3. While you're there, watch when you're eating too

Big meals too close to bedtime are also a bad idea. If your stomach feels full and uncomfortable, it will greatly impair your ability to fall asleep. Try to finish eating for the night at least two hours before going to bed.

4. No screens in the last hour before bedtime

I'll admit this is a hard one to implement. But chances are it will lead to the biggest improvement in the quality of your sleep. Set up your evening routine so the last hour before bedtime is screen-free. Use that time to read (a real book), journal, make your lunch and set out your clothes for the next day. It's the perfect time for pottering.

5. No screens in the bedroom

Studies conclusively show that having your phone on the bedside table affects your sleep. So get rid of it. If it's there because you use it as an alarm clock, get a real alarm clock instead. If it's there so you can answer urgent calls during the night, put it just outside your bedroom door. You'll still hear it out there.

6. Get the temperature right

If you're too hot or too cold at night, you'll find it difficult to get good quality sleep. An ambient temperature of 22-23 degrees Celsius is usually ideal. (You may need to raise or lower it a bit if the air is especially dry or humid.)

7. Exercise every day

Studies have shown that a single bout of moderately intense aerobic exercise both reduces the time it takes to fall asleep and increases the length of sleep. You should be exercising for your mental and cardiovascular health every day anyway, but the fact it also helps you sleep better is a nice bonus.

8. Introduce white noise

If you're a very light sleeper who gets woken by the faintest of noises, consider sleeping with a fan on or using a white noise generator.

9. Quiet your mind

If your anxious, racing mind won't let you fall asleep, and you've tried all the non-pharmaceutical methods to combat it (meditation, mindfulness, journaling, etc.), then consider asking your doctor for some medication to help you sleep.

Anxiety is fuelled by a lack of sleep, and if you don't break the cycle the problem will begin feeding on itself. Of course you don't want to be relying on sleeping tablets or anxiety medication to fall asleep every night. But if a tablet can get you through those particularly rough nights where it's 1am and you're in full panic mode because you're still not asleep, that's pretty helpful.

10. Have a solid bedtime routine

If you can, go to bed at the same time each night and get up at the same time each morning—even on weekends. Our bodies like rhythm. If you keep chopping and changing your sleep routine your body won't know whether it's coming or going, and will struggle to get the rest it needs to truly regenerate.

SHORTCUT 3: MANAGE STRESS BETTER (BE THE EGG, NOT THE POTATO)

In 2010 I had a complete breakdown. Several years of relentless stress from a variety of factors triggered extreme anxiety, which in turn triggered depression and saw me land in a very bad place.

It took a really long time to emerge from that bad place, and by the time I did I knew the equation for me was this:

Stress => Anxiety => Depression

In an act of self-preservation, I began avoiding stress like the plague.

My husband (who had taken over running the business) also knew the equation, so did his best to shield me from stressful situations.

- Narky emails from unhappy clients?
- Worries about the business not bringing in enough income?
- Staff issues?

For years he kept them all to himself.

And I was supremely grateful.

But eventually the universe started sending me a message. It's the only way I can explain seeing this quote *three times* in a two-week period:

> "The same boiling water that softens the potato hardens the egg. It's about what you're made of, not the circumstances."

Yes, it's a bit pithy (like all quotes), and can be taken a few different ways. But I took it as a sign that it was time to put my big-girl-pants on. Time to stop running from challenging situations. Time to start sharing the stress load with my husband again.

By now I was far more resilient than I'd been in 2010. And it wasn't just because I was in a better place mentally. It was also because I'd developed five mindsets to help me manage my stress.

1. Only the controllables can be controlled

In the early years of my business I got into the habit of thinking if I was really organised and could anticipate what people needed before they needed it, and what people thought before they thought it, I could effectively control stressful situations out of my life.

Ha! All this line of thinking achieved was me getting angry at myself whenever a stressful situation arose because I had failed to mind-read the person involved and prevent it before it happened.

Yes, I know. Even I can see how ridiculous it sounds now that I've written it down.

These days I know that no matter how organised we are, challenges will continue to present themselves. But the good thing about life is ...

2. We can always deal with the 'now'

A while ago someone told me I had to read Eckhart Tolle's *The Power of Now* because it would be life changing. And they were right.

Whenever I find myself wanting to go lie down in the corner in the foetal position, I return to a single line from that book:

> *"You can always cope with the now."*

Tolle is right. My strike rate for dealing with the 'now' is 100%. And so is yours. We don't have to like dealing with the 'now'. We just need to know that we can and will.

3. Stress is only as bad as you think it is

A few years ago I saw a TED Talk from Kelly McGonigal titled *How to make stress your friend*. In that talk she shared the results of a study that tracked 30,000 adults in the US. In her talk she shares:

> " ... they started by asking people, "How much stress have you experienced in the last year?" They also asked, "Do you believe that stress is harmful for your health?" And then they used public death records to find out who died.
>
> People who experienced a lot of stress in the previous year had a 43 percent increased risk of dying. But that was only true for the people who also believed that stress is harmful for your health.
>
> People who experienced a lot of stress but did not view stress as harmful were no more likely to die. In fact, they had the lowest risk of dying of anyone in the study, including people who had relatively little stress."

This was a big revelation for me because (ignoring my personal stress => anxiety => depression equation for a moment) I always believed stress was physiologically bad for humans, which justified my avoidance of it.

Listening to McGonigal's talk completely flipped that thinking for me and has totally changed how I respond to stress situations today.

4. Running a business is a privilege

Comparisons can be odious. But sometimes they can also be a nice reality check. These days, if I'm feeling stressed about something, I remind myself how privileged I am to live in a country where a woman has the freedom and tools to start her own business. I'm also privileged to:

- Live in a country where the barriers to starting and running your own business are negligible

- Have a business that's ten years old (given how many businesses fail in their first year)

- Have a business that's surmounted many challenges and been able to evolve in a world that is becoming increasingly digital.

But most of all I'm privileged because, when challenges present themselves, I have the support and resources to take them on. Not everyone has that.

5. Surmounting challenges equals growth

Every challenge I've faced since I first started my business has led to learning and growth that I've been able to put to good use. These days I make better decisions. I've learned to spot the difference between an 'opportunity' and a giant time suck. And I've become a better problem solver and communicator.

In short, all those challenges have made me a better person—personally and professionally.

And if you allow yourself to be more egg than potato when faced with challenges, you'll reap those same benefits too.

SECTION 2: NUMBERS

SHORTCUT 4: YOU ATTRACT WHAT YOU TRACK

Do you like numbers?

I don't. Never have.

And it's something I've always been proud of. Congratulating myself for not knowing off the top of my head how many Facebook fans, Twitter followers or email subscribers I have. Patting myself on the back for doing everything very organically instead of 'being pushy'.

Then I heard someone in a podcast say this:

> "You attract what you track."

That one sentence completely changed my thinking about numbers.

Because when I thought about it, the few numbers I did keep track of (such as daily visitor numbers to the websites I manage) tended to go exactly how I wanted them to. And the numbers I didn't track (such as subscribers to my email list) were a bit all over the place.

And it became clear that I should be paying more attention to two figures in particular:

- Sales figures (given a business needs sales to be profitable)
- Email subscribers (since an email list is the single most powerful marketing tool you can have).

So I decided to do a little experiment.

At the beginning of one particular month I set myself two sales figure goals—one for my design business, and one for my second book.

The result? My business exceeded the sales figure I'd set by 30%. And I hit the book sales figure I'd set halfway through the month.

The best thing was, I didn't hit those figures by being pushy or employing sales tactics I wasn't comfortable with.

It was more that the simple act of setting those targets shifted my focus. When it came to deciding how to spend my time on any given day, sales-generating activities were suddenly at the top of my list (where before, they were somewhere near the bottom). I'd look at my numbers daily, and if they weren't where I wanted them to be I'd do something to get them moving. For example, if I noticed the conversion rate on the lead magnet for our email list had dropped, I'd tweak the copy.

It was such an interesting exercise to see how such a tiny tweak in thinking could have such a significant impact on our bottom line.

It also brought to mind something I once heard from business coach James Schramko in a podcast—this profit formula:

Prospects x conversions = Customers
Customers x $ amount x frequency x % margin = Profit

Applying the 'you attract what you track' thinking I talked about earlier, imagine what would happen if just one of the numbers in that formula went up. Imagine if you could increase:

- Your leads (prospects) *or*
- Your conversion rate *or*
- The price of your product or service ($ amount) *or*
- How often people buy from you (frequency) *or*
- Your margin (by lowering your costs and/or expenses).

It's pretty cool to realise that increasing just one of these numbers would immediately increase your profit.

And the beauty of this 'you attract what you track' concept is you can apply it pretty much anywhere—in both life and business—to anything you want to improve.

SHORTCUT 5: INVOICE SMARTER FOR BETTER CASH FLOW

In the early years of my business (when I was still doing our accounts) I did all our invoicing at the end of each month. This meant if a job finished at the start of a month, it would be 30 days before it was invoiced.

At the time, our payment terms were 30 days. *That* meant that even if the client paid on time it could be 60 days before we received payment. If they didn't pay on time, and I had to chase them up, it could easily blow out to 90 days.

As every business owner knows, cash flow is king. And my invoicing system was putting the business under constant cash flow pressure.

What happens when you're under cash flow pressure?

1. You make bad business decisions (because decisions made from a place of scarcity are seldom good ones).

2. You experience a great deal of stress—the special kind that comes from having no money in the bank to pay your staff and suppliers.

3. You feel angry towards the clients who are behind in paying, which isn't the best thing for client relationships.

So let's fix these things. Here are eight guaranteed shortcuts to better cash flow:

1. Invoice a job as soon as it is finished

If you're a tradesman doing jobs on site, you shouldn't have to go back to the office to send an invoice. You should be able to generate an email invoice right then and there.

If you provide a service-based business at your desk (e.g. design, copywriting, videography, etc.), use a job tracking/time tracking system such as Harvest or Time Doctor so you know how many hours to charge out the second you finish the job.

You should also use an accounting system such as Xero or FreshBooks that lets you invoice quickly and easily, and gives people a link to pay online. FreshBooks actually does time tracking as well, so, for solo operators in particular, it's a winner.

2. Shorten your payment terms

Back in the day, 30-day payment terms were common because most businesses paid by cheque, and it was more efficient to do a cheque run once a month. But, with easy electronic payments (i.e. bank transfers and credit card payments) now accessible to everyone, there's no reason to have 30-day terms unless you're dealing with huge companies or government departments that have very set in stone payment policies.

Personally, I don't think your payment terms should be any longer than seven days. And that's only if you can't get payment as soon as the job is completed (or even before).

Let's say you're a plumber who has just fixed a leaking toilet for someone. You shouldn't have to go back to the office to generate an invoice, then send it out via email (or, god forbid, post) and then wait any amount of days for that person to pay up. With the tools available these days, you should be able to generate an invoice and take payment right there on the spot.

If you're like me and complete a job by providing the client with files or making a website live, make sure you get the final payment before you complete that final step.

Speaking of final payments …

3. Get deposits for large jobs

If you're given a large job that could stretch out for a while, invoice the client 50% before you start and 50% on completion. It means if you spend three months doing 30-40 hours of work, you're not waiting another month before you actually get paid for those hours.

If the job is really big, split the total amount into four payments and clearly indicate the project milestone where each payment needs to be made.

4. If a job stalls, invoice for the work done to date

Sometimes a client brings a job to a standstill by not answering emails/giving you the information or resources you need. But even if they've paid the initial deposit, it doesn't mean you have to wait for them indefinitely.

If the job has been at a standstill for a month or so, let the client know you'll be closing the job and invoicing them for your unpaid hours.

If you don't, you'll be effectively holding credit for your clients, which is another no-no (see next point).

5. Don't hold credit for clients

Just don't.

If a job for a client involves you having to pay another supplier, make sure the client pays for the job up front, or at the very least pays a deposit that covers the supplier's cost.

As an example: whenever we do a print job for a client, we get payment up front. It's too stressful to be in the situation where we pay the printer and then have to chase the client for months to get their payment to cover the supplier's printing cost (and our time).

6. Follow up late payments immediately

If you don't have the time to do this yourself, pay someone to do it for you. Believe me, it will be the best money you've ever spent. If people know they'll get a phone call or email from you if they don't pay on time, they'll make sure you always get paid first. If you get a reputation as being very lax about payment, (which I was, back in the day), the opposite will happen.

7. Have the same terms for everyone

While this isn't practical all the time, it is 99% of the time. Don't make life hard for yourself by making exceptions left, right and centre.

I can say from experience that every time we've made a website live before getting final payment, or ordered and paid for something from a printer without getting a deposit from a client, those are the times we've been left carrying the can.

Yes, it would be nice to think we're great judges of character, and know who we can and can't bend the rules for. But take it from me—we don't.

8. Be very clear about your payment terms

In all of these situations, by being upfront with your client/customer about how and when you'll need to be paid, you'll never have any problems getting paid on time. So have very firm payment terms, make them clear to clients before they engage you, and then make sure you stick to them.

SHORTCUT 6: MAKE IT SUPER-EASY FOR PEOPLE TO BUY FROM YOU

I've said it before and I'm sure I'll say it again many, many times:

> *The biggest competitor all businesses face is not another business. Our number one competitor is apathy.*

You need only look at your own behaviour to understand.

You need to see your physio.

Or get a haircut.

Or organise t-shirts for the fun run you've roped everyone into doing at work.

But right now, it's easier to do nothing than pick up the phone and make that physiotherapist appointment, right? And it's a heck of a lot easier to do nothing than to try and figure out where you can get a bunch of t-shirts printed up.

How can you use this knowledge of your own behaviour to get your clients to buy from you faster?

Make their next step so easy it overrides the ease of doing nothing.

- If you're a physiotherapist—instead of making people ring your clinic and having days and times thrown at them by a receptionist, let them book their appointment themselves online.

- If you're an online store—can you create a one-page checkout? Can you offer PayPal as well as credit card payments so that if I'm ready to buy I can simply login to PayPal instead of having to go downstairs to get my wallet? (I can easily remember my PayPal password, but I can never remember my credit card details.)

- If you deliver the ingredients for meals—can you offer a subscription service? Most people find it easier to keep a subscription going than cancel it.

When we build websites for clients, there are MANY steps in the process where apathy can cause things to stall. This means we're constantly refining our systems to make each step easier for them.

And it benefits both of us—we get the job done and get paid faster. And the client gets their website finished and live faster too!

SECTION 3: PRODUCTIVITY

SHORTCUT 7: GET UP EARLIER (AS OPPOSED TO 'EARLY')

I'm sure you've read those articles about the morning habits of successful people. It seems they all get up at 5am each day and do heaps of useful stuff before the rest of the world emerges from their beds.

And I will say—if this is your bag (it's definitely mine), then great! Getting up earlier than the rest of the world is a brilliant way to be more productive.

But, I understand that for most people, the pros of getting up at 5am are not outweighed by the cons. So the thing I want to highlight in this particular shortcut is the difference between getting up *early*, and getting up *earlier* than you have to.

I know a lot of people who roll out of bed with just enough time to jump in the shower, get ready, and head out the door to catch the bus/jump in the car. While it may seem 'efficient' what it really means is they're under pressure from the moment they start the day. And if:

- Their cat has thrown up in the kitchen or
- They discover none of their shirts are ironed or

- They space out for a minute too long in the shower

their morning goes from rushed to frantic in a heartbeat.

If your morning is rushed and frantic, chances are good that the rest of your day will pan out that way as well. Being rushed puts us in 'fight or flight' mode and elevates the level of cortisol (a stress hormone) in our bodies. Studies have shown that consistently elevated cortisol levels can trigger:

- Anxiety
- Depression
- Digestive problems
- Headaches
- Heart disease
- Sleep problems
- Weight gain
- Memory and concentration impairment.

And that's not exactly ideal.

Now, let's talk about the concept of getting up earlier (as opposed to early).

You'll be amazed what a difference setting your alarm for as little as 15 minutes earlier can make to your life. Instead of having to leap out of bed and straight into the shower, you can now slowly wander into the kitchen and spend ten minutes flicking through the paper or scrolling through Instagram before your shower.

If you get up 30 minutes earlier you can wander into the kitchen, make yourself a cuppa and something to eat, and enjoy breakfast while reading the paper or scrolling through Facebook before your shower.

This whole 'getting up earlier' thing has two benefits:

1. If you do have to deal with a contingency, you have the time to do it without sending your blood pressure into the stratosphere.

2. When you leave the house, you feel ready to take on the day rather than being thrown unceremoniously into it.

So, how is this a shortcut to business success?

Firstly, it makes you a nicer person. People like doing business with people, especially people they like. But it's hard to be your best self when you start every day feeling frantic.

Secondly, it makes you a clearer thinker. And when you're thinking clearly you can make better decisions, and solve problems more creatively and effectively.

How do you find your way to getting up earlier if you're not a morning person?

1. Understand that no-one really likes getting up in the morning—even the most avid 'morning people' don't jump out of bed when their alarms go off singing 'Woo hoo! Let's do this.' So don't think that because you're not jumping out of bed with glee that this whole 'getting up earlier' thing isn't working for you.

2. Start small. Don't suddenly try to become the person that wakes up at 5am to meditate, write in their journal and exercise before starting their day. As I mentioned before, getting up just 15 minutes earlier can make a huge difference to your day. Start with that, and then as it becomes habit and you start to enjoy its positive effects think about getting up a little earlier.

SHORTCUT 8: PRACTISE STRATEGIC PROCRASTINATION

It sounds almost too good to be true, doesn't it? I'm telling all you procrastinators that your pathological bad habit can be a shortcut to success.

Well, yes it can. But I'm not talking about your regular variety of procrastination here. You need to be strategic about it.

How? Try these three mindsets/methods:

1. Understand just because you can do something quickly doesn't mean you should

When it comes to email, I used to be like Quick Draw McGraw. If anything dropped into my inbox that I could deal with quickly (via a reply or an action), I'd do it straight away. I loved it because my inbox was my to-do list, and this kept it nice and clean. Clients loved it because they got instant action on their requests.

I think we can all see this was actually a bit of a problem:

- I'd spend my entire day keeping my inbox 'clean'
- The more I responded quickly to clients, the more they'd email me whenever they ran into trouble.

A little while ago I started checking my email only three times a day. I hated it (which is a story for another day), but this little productivity experiment highlighted something very interesting. When I opened up my inbox after two or three hours, it was staggering how often an email from someone saying, "Help!" was quickly followed by another one saying, "It's okay. I figured it out".

What this showed me was that, even though I could respond to an email instantly, it didn't mean I should. By strategically procrastinating about answering certain types of emails, issues often became non-issues without me needing to get involved.

And the same rule applies to most 'urgencies' out there. If left alone, many of them become non-urgent, or even non-existent.

2. Practise productive procrastination

Say you're writing a blog post or a report, and you get stuck. What do you do? Well, if you're like me you head to Facebook to 'give your mind a rest'.

And we all know what happens next: You fall down the Facebook rabbit hole, watch a few videos, laugh at a few memes, come back to your desk and ... discover that you're still stuck.

In situations like this, I've found a short walk can be a highly productive way to procrastinate. Why does it work? Well, as the saying goes, "If you can see far and wide, you can think far and wide". Getting away from your desk and heading outside opens up your mind to new possibilities.

And the beauty of walking as a productive procrastination strategy is it doesn't even need to be a long one. Just walking around the block, or even up and down a stairwell, will clear both your mind and the roadblock that made you leave your desk in the first place.

3. Give important things time to marinate

Got an important decision to make, or an important pitch to prepare? Then do yourself a favour. Do a brain dump to get all your ideas out, and then walk away from it for 24 hours.

In that 24-hour period your subconscious will process all of your thoughts, and provide you with amazing clarity around said thoughts.

The end result is always a cracking resolution or outcome—one you could never achieve by forcing yourself to sit down and get everything done in one go.

SHORTCUT 9: STOP STARTING AGAIN AND EAT THE FROG FIRST

It's time to start work, so you sit down at your computer. As you sip your coffee you check your email, answer the items you can, make note of what needs to be added to today's to-do list, file anything that can be filed, and then before you know it ...

Half an hour has passed.

You feel like you deserve a reward for your efforts, so you head to Facebook for a 'quick break'. By the time you've clicked through all your notifications (must get rid of that annoying red number) you've been at your desk for an hour.

Time for a toilet break.

And since you're up, you may as well grab a quick cuppa.

By the time you get back to your desk more emails have arrived, and you figure you may as well deal with those before you start doing your work.

The same pattern repeats itself: you check your emails, head to Facebook for a much-needed 'mental break', get lost down the rabbit hole, leave your desk for another much-needed break, get back to your desk ...

Lather, rinse, repeat.

We all have a 'start' routine we go through when we sit down at our desks to start work. And it usually involves 'clearing our plate' of all the crappy little jobs (such as getting on top of our emails) before we start on the real/meaty work for the day. Before we know it we've gone through our start routine three times, it's lunchtime, and we haven't actually 'done' anything yet.

And when we get back from lunch we do it all over again. Now it's two in the afternoon, and we still haven't done any real work for the day. So we finally put our heads down and get stuff done.

Or at least try to.

Unfortunately, when our productivity was at its peak we were too busy dealing with emails to take advantage of it. Now even the small jobs seem to take forever. So what do we focus on?

The smallest jobs we can find.

And the big jobs? Well, they're still there on our to-do list. We figure we'll tackle those jobs 'tomorrow when we're feeling fresher' but guess what? This same pattern will repeat itself tomorrow too.

Here's what I know about those big jobs: the longer we put them off, the bigger they become in our minds. And eventually they become so big that we never do them.

The worst thing is, those big hard jobs are usually the ones that help us build our business:

- The proposal to a new client or partner
- The book you keep meaning to write
- The website revamp you know is long overdue.

So how do we get better at making time for these business-building jobs?

1. Be aware of your 'start' routine, and be honest about how much it drains your productivity.

2. Set a mandate to go through your 'start' routine once only (if that), and then 'eat a frog' before you do anything else (Facebook, other smaller, easier jobs, etc.)

What do I mean by 'eat a frog'? I'll let Brian Tracy (the one who popularised the concept) explain:

> *"Mark Twain once said that if the first thing you do each morning is eat a live frog, you can go through the day with the satisfaction of knowing that is probably the worst thing that's going to happen to you all day long. Your 'frog' is your biggest, most important task, the one you are most likely to procrastinate on."*

Once you start tackling the business-building tasks I mentioned earlier as the first point of order, you'll be amazed how quickly they move from 'to-do' to 'done'. Not to mention how much earlier you'll get to reap the benefits of having done them.

Your days will also become more enjoyable because you won't be spending the afternoon trying (and failing) to muster enough willpower to do the hard stuff. Instead you'll be spending that time doing jobs that are both easier on the mind and a lot more fun.

SHORTCUT 10: RE-THINK MEETINGS

There are two types of people in this world: those who love meetings, and those who loathe them. I'm firmly in the 'loathe' category because I value productivity and efficiency. And nothing kills those things quite like a meeting.

And it's not just me who thinks so. A 2013 report by Atlassian estimated that US businesses were wasting $37 billion a year on pointless meetings, and that the average employee spends more than 31 hours a month in unnecessary meetings.

What were the people doing at these meetings?

- 91% daydreamed
- 45% felt overwhelmed
- 73% did other work
- 39% fell asleep
- 47% felt the meeting was a complete waste of time.

I don't know anyone in business who has time to waste these days. We all have more work to do and less time to do it in. So what can we do to make meetings a little less painful? I have three suggestions:

1. Reduce the number of meetings in your life

- Never meet to have a discussion you could have via email or over the phone.

- Never meet to share information that's already documented and can be read.

- Never travel to a meeting you could have over Skype.

2. Make the meetings you do attend more productive

- Make sure the person running the meeting is someone who can keep a firm handle on things. They need to make sound judgement calls on when to let people talk something out, and when to nip something in the bud to keep the meeting moving along.

- Make sure there's an agenda, and that it's been circulated before the meeting. Even if someone asks you to meet them for coffee so they can 'get your thoughts on something', ask them to send through some talking points.

- Ruthlessly stick to the agenda. If the conversation goes off-topic, tell those involved to arrange another meeting to have their discussion—no matter how useful it might be.

- Never include agenda items that could be discussed more fruitfully in another way. In our Swish Design meetings we used to get each person to state the jobs they were currently working on, and for whom. This information could have easily been compiled ahead of time and quickly scanned by everyone before the meeting. Instead, we would spend 30-40 minutes listening to each person state every job they were working on, comment on certain jobs, and then watching things go tangential whenever a comment sparked an unrelated conversation.

- Always set a firm start and finish time. How many 10am meetings actually start at 10:15am by the time everyone grabs a coffee or goes to the toilet? How many meetings go for hours because an undefined finish time gives people license to labour points and discuss things ad infinitum?

- Make sure everyone is clear on any action items they receive during the meeting.

- Have shorter, more frequent meetings. The longer the gap between meetings, the more likely they'll go for hours. Why? Because everyone will be desperate to get their idea or point across if they think it will be weeks or even months before they get another chance to be heard.

3. Re-think the sit-down meeting

- If there are only two of you, have a walking meeting. They're more productive (walking stimulates our brains), less awkward (you're not staring at each other across the table), and more efficient because there's a definite start and finish time (i.e. once you're back where you started, the meeting is over).

- If there's a large group of you, have a standing meeting. Ideal for short, sharp meetings, it helps ensure everyone stays ruthlessly on point. (No-one likes standing any longer than they have to.)

SHORTCUT 11: EMBRACE ROUTINE

Routines are boring, right?

Monotonous. Restrictive. Inflexible. Creatively stifling.

I often hear routine-averse folk use these words as they tell me how much they love the freedom of taking each day as it comes.

And you know what? If it's working out for them, then more power to them.

But for the most part, what I see in these people is frustration. They're not achieving their business goals, and can't quite figure out why.

But I can.

A lack of routine makes us reactive. It puts us on edge, and in constant 'fight or flight' mode. It adds to our decision-making load and tires us out mentally, which leads to poor decision making, particularly at the back end of each day.

Most of all, a lack of routine means we just aren't as productive as we could be.

Routines don't have to be tyrannical masters. They can be loyal servants too:

- They reduce cognitive load (the amount we have to think).

- They reduce reactivity and stress.

- Instead of starting each day with a blank slate (which can be overwhelming), routines provide a structure around which to build your day.

- When days go pear-shaped, instead of this causing a 'cascade of shitfulness' as I like to call it, routines allow you to get things back under control quickly and with a minimum of pain.

But here's the best thing about routines. Since they increase our productivity, they can be used to intentionally create pockets of time and space in our days where we can 'do whatever we want'. Where we can be free to dream and just 'be' without that nagging sense of 'I should be doing something more useful here'.

This is such a powerful gift to your business because it's those pockets of 'unstructured' time that will allow you to innovate and come up with the ideas that will take your business to the next level.

But you'll never get to experience the power of those pockets of time if you don't first invoke the power of routine.

So how do you go about building routines into your days?

Remember: you're not creating a routine *for* your day. You're adding routines *to* your day.

As an example, here's the routine I follow in the morning:

My morning routine

4:15am: Wake up, drink two big glasses of water while browsing Instagram and making a coffee.

4:30am: Quickly scan emails and delete the crap.

4:45am: Write for 45 minutes to an hour.

5:30am-ish: Do morning exercise (running, rowing, walking or CrossFit).

6:30am: Get home from exercise, make my seven-year-old's school lunch.

7am: Get toddler up and make a breakfast smoothie for myself and my husband.

7:30am: Tidy up kitchen, have a shower and get dressed.

8:30am: School drop-off

9:00am: Start work

Here's why my morning routine is so important:

- It ensures I get some quiet time to myself every day.

- It ensures I get quality time to write every day. (My energy levels for writing are highest in the morning when no-one else is around or wants to talk to me.)

- It ensures I do some form of exercise every day. (As mentioned in Section 1 of this book, daily exercise is crucial for good energy levels.)

- It ensures I'm in a good mood when the rest of my family wakes up so I can deal with any of their grumpiness with good humour.

- It ensures our mornings are chilled, which means we're all calm when we walk out the door to start our days. (Remember: the way you leave the house in the morning has a huge effect on how the rest of your day pans out.)

- It gives my brain a break. Instead of spending any time in those morning hours trying to figure out what I should do next, I'm pretty much operating on autopilot.

My morning routine is important. But I also have other routines I follow throughout the day.

For example, embedded in that morning routine is both a **writing routine** and an **exercise routine**. Having these two routines means I don't have to waste willpower trying to motivate myself to write or exercise. I just do them.

You already know I have the same thing for breakfast every morning (green smoothie). Not having to decide what to have for breakfast every morning has freed up an incredible amount of mental space.

We also have an **afternoon routine** in our house that starts when I get home from the afternoon school run and finishes with me putting dinner on the table.

Then we have an **evening routine** that revolves around the kids having baths and then us chilling out as a family before the kids go to bed. (Yes, we even schedule 'chill out' time into our evenings.)

Once the kids are in bed I have a **'get ready for the next day' routine** that makes me feel on top of the next day and thus helps me sleep better.

On the weekends I have a Sunday afternoon **'get ready for the next week' routine** that's all about feeling on top of the week ahead.

One of the biggest advantages I find with these routines is that they eliminate most surprises. I don't find out at 8am that there's no bread in the fridge to make my son's school lunch and I'm never shocked to find I have an early meeting scheduled for 8:30am.

By having routines you can identify anything that's *out of routine* much earlier, and notify anyone it affects *before* it becomes an issue.

So how do you create a routine?

Well, first you need to know your desired outcome.

- The desired outcome of my morning routine is that instead of our mornings being full of angst and people yelling at each other because, "I can't believe you don't have your shoes on yet", we can all walk out of the house and head off to school, day care and the office feeling chilled and ready for the day.
- The desired outcome of my writing routine is to ensure I write at least 750 words every day.
- The desired outcome of my exercise routine is to ensure I move my body for at least 20 minutes every day.
- The desired outcome of my afternoon routine is to set things up for the evening routine.
- The desired outcome of my evening routine is for us all to have some quality time together as a family.
- The desired outcome of my 'get ready for the next day' routine is to feel on top of the next day so I sleep well that night.

Once you know the desired outcome, you can create the steps necessary to achieve it. For example, the steps involved in my 'get ready for the next day' routine are:

- Checking my diary to see what's on.
- Putting out my exercise clothes for the next morning, along with the clothes I'll be wearing for the day.

- Moving the meat for dinner the following evening from the freezer to the fridge.
- Doing a final tidy to ensure I can lay down on the couch to chill out before bed without feeling agitated by seeing mess out of the corner of my eye, and that I can wake up the next morning without being faced with dishes in the sink.

The most important thing with any routine is being able to repeat it over and over again. If you're struggling to execute a given routine, then either you're trying to fit too much into the time you've allocated or your energy levels are too low.

And the best thing about routines? When 'things happen' that derail your entire day, it's not a problem because you get to start again fresh the following day. And your routines provide a way to 'reset' rather than feeling you're starting from scratch.

SHORTCUT 12:
PRACTISE THE ONE-MINUTE RULE

You need to book a time to see your accountant. Should you do it now, or later?

You notice the light bulb in the toilet has blown. Should you change it now, or later?

The photocopier is out of paper. Should you refill it now, or later?

You take your dirty coffee cup into the kitchen. Should you wash it now, or later?

You pay a bill, and make a note on the printout that it's been paid. Should you file it now, or later?

Countless things like this crop up over the course of a day.

Countless.

And we waste a huge amount of time and energy trying to decide "Should I do this now, or later?" with all of them. (Remember, every decision we have to make over the course of a day saps our willpower, and affects our ability to make good decisions later in the day.)

What if there was a quick and easy way to decide whether to do something now, or later? What if there was a way to save a big chunk of that energy?

Well, there is. It's called the one-minute rule. And it's absurdly easy to apply.

Whenever you catch yourself doing the 'now or later' thing, if it will take you less than one minute to do, then do it now.

Seriously. Just do it.

Why? Here are three great reasons:

1. It will eliminate the situation where you've flicked the light switch for the fifteenth time only to remember, "Oh, yeah. The bulb's blown". (At which point a tiny job suddenly seems larger than it is and starts taking up even more head space).

2. It will reduce the frustration you feel for not having taken care of it the first time you noticed.

3. It will end the debate you're having with yourself about doing stupid little jobs, and free up some valuable head space because you're no longer debating with yourself.

SECTION 4: MARKETING

SHORTCUT 13: LEVERAGE THE POWER OF STORYTELLING

Many years ago, when my friends and I didn't have much disposable income, one of them bought a new pillow for the princely sum of $100. When I stared at her in shock (it seemed like a lot to me), she quickly justified the purchase:

"As the sales girl said to me, this is something I use every single night, so the price per use is tiny, and also, good sleep is crucial to our health, so it's basically an investment in my health."

Fast forward 20-odd years, where my husband and I now pay our finance guys a retainer each month. It's not a huge amount, but it certainly adds up over the course of a year. Whenever we're called on to justify the expense, this is what we say:

"The amount we pay over the course of the year is easily paid back by the fact they help ensure everything we do financially is as tax-efficient as possible, and that we're making sound, long-term financial decisions."

We all need to be able to justify the purchase decisions we make—to ourselves (there's nothing worse than buyer's remorse), and often to others.

And this is where the power of storytelling comes into play.

For many of us, the value of our product or service is hard to define. Giving someone a story they can tell themselves (and others) about the money they're spending helps overcome any qualms they may have about spending it.

How do we do that? I suggest doing three things:

1. State what you do very clearly on the home page of your website

- The online note-taking app Evernote tells people it helps them 'Remember Everything'.
- WP Curve, a WordPress support service, says it helps remove your WordPress pains.
- My design business tells people we help them tell their business story better.

People won't necessarily use the exact words we give them. But those words will provide a great starting point for the story they'll eventually tell themselves and others about us. So take advantage of being in control of that starting point.

2. Get great client testimonials

We all know why people might find it hard to justify spending money with us. It might be because:

- We're expensive.
- They're not exactly sure what we can do for them.
- They can't understand why they'd pay us to do something they could do themselves.

This is where client testimonials can help immensely. Sure, we can tell people how great we are at what we do, and how we're worth the hefty price tag because we're 'different' or 'better'. But when our clients do it, their story has far more power than any story we could tell.

That's why you should make the effort to collect customer testimonials, and then place them front and centre on your website.

3. Do what you say you'll do

The message here is very simple: don't make promises you can't keep.

There's a service provider in my life right now who, over the course of the past six months, has given me countless assurances that certain things will be done by certain dates. They've failed to deliver on those assurances. Every. Single. Time.

You can only imagine the story I'm telling myself and others about this service provider at the moment.

You can't always get this one right—things do happen. But it's such an easy way to set yourself apart from the crowd, as most people don't seem capable of doing what they say they'll do.

So ... why wouldn't you?

SHORTCUT 14: MARKET YOUR BUSINESS IN 10 MINUTES A DAY

You've got a list, right? One that contains all the big ideas you have for spreading the word about your business. And I bet once you get on top of your workload you'll set aside an entire day to action one of those big ideas.

There's just one problem: that day never comes, does it? If it does, it's only because your phone has stopped ringing.

I can say this from experience: one of the worst times to start marketing your business is when the work has dried up. That's why I'm a big fan of spending a little time (I'm talking ten minutes here) doing something small every day. It's realistic. It's ongoing. And thanks to its cumulative effect, can build something very big for you over time.

What can you achieve in ten minutes a day (or less) that will help grow your business? Lots.

Here are 25 ideas to get you started:

1. Email a client you haven't heard from for a while with an article you think might interest them.

2. Leave a thoughtful comment on something someone has posted on Facebook.

3. Congratulate a friend on their work anniversary on LinkedIn.

4. Read an article a friend or colleague has just published on their blog.

5. Share that article with your social networks.

6. Leave a thoughtful comment on their blog post—one that adds something meaningful to the conversation (this shows your expertise, your personality, and gives you a nice backlink to your website too).

7. Introduce two people you think would work well together (with their permission, of course).

8. Join a relevant business group on Facebook or small business discussion forum.

9. Visit those communities at least once a week, find a discussion you can contribute to meaningfully, and leave a considered comment. (If you can't find one, don't just comment for the sake of it.)

10. Send a 'Thank You' card to someone who's done something nice for you.

11. Send a congratulations card to someone who's achieved something, no matter how small. Receiving nice things in the mail is a real thrill for people these days, and it's an easy way to make a good impression.

12. Email someone who's made a positive impact on your life via something they've said, written or advice they've given—and tell them about the impact they've made.

13. Leave a review for your favourite podcast on iTunes.

14. Leave a review on Amazon for that great business book you've read.

15. Read up on one of the speakers at the next conference you're going to.

16. Look up the contributor guidelines for a business website you could write for.

17. Pitch a keynote idea to the person who runs the conference you attend every year.

18. Do a ten-minute brain dump of a business book you could write.

19. Email a client who loves your work and ask if they'll write you a testimonial.

20. Make a quick list of the five questions clients ask you the most, and choose one as the topic for your next blog post.

21. Check your LinkedIn profile and ensure it's up to date.

22. Read through your About page (the second most visited site on your website after your home page) and check that it's more about the person reading it than it is about you.

23. Test out the contact form on your website to make sure it's working.

24. Sign up for your own email newsletter and see if there's anything in the sign-up process a subscriber might find jarring.

25. Pretend you're a client and do a walk-through of your office. Do you see anything that needs tidying or fixing up?

Remember: lots of ten-minute actions, especially relationship-building actions, will add up to something much larger than you can ever achieve by setting aside a day to do something 'big'. Especially considering that day seldom comes.

> Would you like a daily prompt and some accountability around doing one of these ten-minute relationship-building actions each day? Head to **swishdesign.com.au/accountable** for more.

SHORTCUT 15: GET PEOPLE TO CRAVE YOU

If you're a small business owner, you probably spend a lot of time trying to figure out how to sell yourself and get customers/clients to understand your value. But having to constantly explain what you're bringing to the table with your services gets exhausting, doesn't it?

What if there was another way?

In his book *The Power of Habit*, Charles Duhigg explains the simple feedback loop that drives habits.

- First comes the cue—something that triggers a behaviour
- Second comes the routine—the actual behaviour triggered by the cue
- Third comes the reward—the payoff.

As an example, let's say you want to start a running habit. Your cue could be lacing up your shoes, which should then trigger the routine (behaviour) of going for a run. And at the end comes the reward—a hit of endorphins or sense of accomplishment.

But here's the thing. As Duhigg points out in *The Power of Habit*:

> " ... countless studies have shown that a cue and a reward, on their own, aren't enough for a new habit to last. Only when your brain starts expecting the reward—craving the endorphins or sense of accomplishment—will it become automatic to lace up your jogging shoes each morning. The cue, in addition to triggering a routine, must also trigger a craving for the reward to come."

Fascinating, right?

So how do you make your marketing effortless? By creating a situation where, when a certain cue presents itself, your clients crave YOU.

Some examples:

- If I tweak my hamstring during a run, I crave the relief from applying my preferred brand of kinesiology tape to the injured muscle.
- If I'm fretting about my finances, I crave the peace of mind our finance guys provide once they've given our numbers the once-over.

These people don't need to market themselves to me all the time. Their service, and the efficacy of their product, means I think of them the second I find myself hankering for the 'relief' they can provide. Calling on them the second I crave that relief has become a lasting habit for me.

So what does this mean for you?

Well, first you have to decide what craving you can satisfy. Then you have to demonstrate (through amazing service) that you're the fastest path to satisfying that craving.

For example, the craving my design business wants to satisfy is the feeling of "I just don't know where to start with this (website/design related) thing. Really, I just want someone to take it off my hands entirely". And the only way we can do that is by showing up every day and doing what we're good at: solving these kinds of problems for our clients so they can focus on what they're good at.

It's the same way my local laundromat satisfies my craving for fewer chores on the weekend. (They'll wash, dry and fold a giant basket of clothes for $25!)

And it's the same way the deli down the road satisfies my craving for something that's both healthy *and* will quickly fill my belly.

So now it's over to you. What craving can you satisfy for people? And how will you make sure you're the first person they think of when they have a problem you can solve?

SECTION 5: MINDSET

SHORTCUT 16: STOP SAVING, START INVESTING – IN YOURSELF

There's a saying:

"Never jump over dollars to get to dimes."

What does this look like in business? Essentially, it's being frugal and saving money wherever you can, rather than investing in yourself and your business to bring in bigger dollars down the track.

This behaviour usually comes from a place of scarcity, and looks like this:

- Refusing to hire a bookkeeper because you know how to do your own books.
- Umming and ahhing about going to a conference because you don't have the cash and will have to pay for it on your credit card.
- Thinking, "Why would I pay this person for a consultation when I can read their blog?"

Here's what I know about each of those scenarios:

Yes, when I first hired a bookkeeper it cost me money.

But it also freed up countless hours, not to mention my head space. I could make far more money from those freed up hours than the bookkeeper cost me. And the benefit of always knowing our cash position and having daily cash flows on hand has helped my business in ways I can't put a price on.

The first conference I went to was a fair investment to make, in what was at the time, a hobby at best.

But invest I did, and that investment has paid off many times over since then. (I've made some great friends and formed many wonderful friendships online. But there's no substitute for the level of connection you get from meeting people in real life and having proper conversations with them.)

Conversations from that first conference led to me working with some of Australia's biggest bloggers as a designer and adviser. I've since been invited back to speak about writing, design and website tech. Attending the event every year has helped me cement relationships with people who've helped with my writing career. And a chance encounter at the event one year led to me landing my dream job as Editor of *Flying Solo*—Australia's largest online publication for solo and micro businesses.

Not every conference will be a game-changer for you or your business, so you do have to choose wisely. But if you attend an event that either contains like-minded people or people who might want to hire you, and use those conferences to create meaningful connections with people, it would be hard not to see a return on your investment.

I've avidly read the blogs of many smart people over the years.

And I've taken away a lot from all that reading. But what people share on their blogs is (necessarily) quite general. So whenever I've had the chance to buy an hour of these people's time, I've taken it.

Being able to take their knowledge and apply it to my *specific* situation has always been money well spent. In fact, I'd say this particular shortcut has helped me achieve my business goals faster than anything else.

And there's another advantage to paying for someone's time. If they're an influencer in the circles you like to move in, you now have their attention. They know who you are. Which is another thing that's very hard to put a price on.

Bottom line

If your sole pathway to a profitable bottom line is to save every penny, I doubt you will ever be truly successful. Start betting on yourself by investing in yourself and the future of your business. Because let's face it: how often do you get to bet on an outcome you can influence so directly?

SHORTCUT 17: PUT YOURSELF OUT THERE— LEARN THE ART OF ASKING

Someone once asked me for advice about 'getting themselves out there' a bit more. They asked me what I'd done to be 'seen' as much as I am.

At first I didn't know what they were talking about. So they clarified that it seemed I was 'everywhere':

- My second book *Practical Perfection* had gotten some great press including write-ups in *Forbes* and *The Herald Sun* and a guest post on *Mamamia* (a huge women's website in Australia).
- I was the editor of *Flying Solo*—Australia's largest online publication for solo and micro business owners—with both a monthly column and a weekly email column.
- I was being asked to speak at conferences and business events.
- If people were looking for a designer for their blog in online groups, my name often came up.
- My two podcasts were getting great traction.

They wanted to know what my 'secret' was.

Well, after giving it a lot of thought, I decided it all came down to this personal mantra of mine:

> "If you don't ask, the answer is always 'No.'"

Now here's the irony of this: I hate asking. For anything.

Deep down, I've always felt that my general awesomeness should be obvious to everyone. That I should be the first person anyone would consider when looking for someone to:

- Interview
- Profile
- Send business to
- Speak about anything I'm good at.

It took a while, but the reality of the situation eventually sank in. If I sat around all day waiting for people to notice me and ask me to do stuff, I'd be waiting a long time.

To become 'known' I had to learn the art of asking, and to put myself out there a bit more.

That *Flying Solo* Editor role? It first came up in 2012. I was in no position to take it on at the time, but I knew *Flying Solo* was an organisation I wanted to work for in the future should the opportunity ever arise. So I applied for the role, and got an interview. They offered to do the interview via Skype, but I wanted to put myself in front of them in a literal sense. So I flew to Sydney and back in a day to do just that.

I didn't get the Editor job back then (phew). But when it came up again two years later, who was one of the people they approached? Me. Who was much better placed to take on the role? Me. Who got the role that time? Me.

In 2015 I presented at the ProBlogger conference (Australia's largest conference for online influencers), and in 2016 I was asked to present again. Why? Because I've pitched a session to them every year since 2010. I'm a hardcore introvert, so most people assume I hate speaking. I don't. I actually love it. But the ProBlogger team wouldn't have known that if I wasn't always pitching to them.

What about writing? In the past six years I've received invaluable guidance, mentorship and feedback about the craft from people I hugely respect and admire—all because I asked. If I'd never asked, I'd be only half the writer I am today.

Everything good that's ever come my way in a professional sense has come from me being willing to put myself out there. Nothing has ever come my way because someone 'happened to notice me being awesome.' It might happen once in a blue moon to other people, but it has never happened to me.

In business we're afraid to ask about so much.

- We're afraid to ask for the sale because we might seem desperate.
- We're afraid to ask for referrals and testimonials because we might seem too needy.
- We're afraid to ask for feedback because we're afraid of hearing something negative.
- We're afraid to ask for help because we don't want to dent our façade of having it all together.

And it all adds up to a business that isn't reaching its full potential.

If you never ask, the answer is always "No".

But … what if they *do* say no?

I can honestly say I rarely hear a flat out "No".

- I hear "Not right now".
- I hear "Not that, but what about this?"
- I hear "Not right for me, but maybe try this person".

All of these responses start a dialogue, and that dialogue gives me the information I need for a "Yes" further down the track.

If you never ask, you'll never get that information.

But what if you're not very good at asking? How do you get good at it?

Here are the rules I abide by:

1. Never ask unless you're really clear on what you want

I never send vague requests like, "Can we catch up for coffee?"

I'm always very specific: "Can I spend an hour with you to find out where you think I might be going wrong with my pitching strategy?"

2. Make sure you're asking the right person

When I was pitching session ideas for the ProBlogger conference, I wasn't pitching them to Darren Rowse (the big boss). I was pitching them to the people who were responsible for scheduling the conference program.

Asking the wrong person means you haven't done your research, and makes you look like an amateur.

3. Time it right

Once there was a particular person I wanted to get feedback from about my writing. When I emailed her she was on book deadline, and obviously unable to help. Silly me. As a fan, I should have known she was on book deadline, and timed my request better. I blew that particular chance.

4. Try and make it a win-win

Admittedly this isn't always possible. But at one point I was once again emailing someone about getting some mentoring from them. (I've emailed a lot of different people about mentoring!) I knew they needed help with their website design, so I offered to help them with that in exchange for an hour-long chat on Skype. Happily, they saw it as a fair swap. And they continue to mentor me to this day.

5. Don't write an essay

If you're writing to tell someone how they've changed your life, and you don't need anything in return other than, "Hey, thanks for letting me know", then go nuts and send your whole life story.

But if you want something from them, keep it short. Really short.

One sentence to explain why you think they can help you.

One sentence to explain the help you'd like them to give you.

That's it.

6. Don't ask for more than one thing at a time

Don't send lists to people. Not even people you know really well. It's easy for them to say "Yes" to one thing. But three? That will give them pause, and make it easy for them to say, "I'd love to help, but I just don't have the time to do all these things for you right now".

7. Ask for small before you ask for big

It would be inappropriate for me to pitch an idea for an opening keynote to a conference organiser if I've only ever presented to small community groups.

It would be inappropriate for me to ask for a regular column at a publication I've never even written a one-off article for.

Asking for big before you've asked for small just makes you look silly and makes getting a "Yes" from that person much harder—even for the small stuff. (When they've said "No" to you once, it's easier to say it again next time.) While there's definitely a place in life for audacity, be very discerning with your timing on that kind of thing.

SHORTCUT 18:
BE WILLING TO NARROW YOUR FOCUS

Your friend shows you her kick-arse Instagram strategy …

A webinar about sales funnels demonstrates exactly how powerful they can be when they're done right …

You read a case study about a business owner who writes one piece of content each week and repurposes it for eight different social media platforms …

All these things work. They all produce great results.

But here's the thing no-one is telling you:

> "Just because something works doesn't mean you're obliged to do it."

Trust me when I tell you I know how hard this is to put into practice. I hang around with some very clever online business people. The stuff they come up with for their own businesses is insanely effective, and they're always very generous in sharing their strategies with their friends. The thing is, if I tried to implement every amazing thing people shared with me, I'd start drowning in overwhelm very quickly.

So how do you decide where you should focus your efforts? Let's take another look at that profit formula I shared in Shortcut 4:

Prospects x conversions = Customers
Customers x $ amount x frequency x % margin = Profit

Here's the powerful thing about this formula: you only need to increase one of those numbers to increase your bottom line (profit).

So you can focus on doing *just one* of these things:

- Creating a better lead magnet for your website (to increase prospects)
- Fine-tuning your sales process (to increase conversions)
- Putting up your prices (to increase the $ amount)
- Offering complimentary products/services or a monthly recurring service (to increase the frequency)
- Reducing your costs (to increase the percentage margin.)

Knowing your current focus makes it a LOT easier to choose which of the hundreds of amazing 'these really work' strategies you'll implement first. And what's even better is that once you've implemented one, and it's humming along nicely for you, you can move on to the next. The compound effect of this will yield far greater results (both financially and mental health-wise) than trying to implement six new strategies at once, and doing all of them badly.

Besides, if you implement six strategies at once how can you measure each strategy's effectiveness? You can't. And as you know from Shortcut 4 in this book, it's hard to attract what you can't track.

SHORTCUT 19: SET YOURSELF UP TO MAKE BETTER DECISIONS

The alarm goes off, and you lie there for a few minutes. Should you go to the gym today or tomorrow?

You decide tomorrow is fine.

You lie there a bit longer. Should you get out of bed now? Or just lay there snoozing for another 20 minutes? If you get up now you'll have time for breakfast. If not, you'll have to either skip it or grab something unhealthy from that lunch bar near the office.

You decide you've been eating too much crap lately. So you get up and wander into the kitchen.

What will you have for breakfast? Can you be bothered making eggs? No. Porridge it is, then.

Shower time. No meetings today, so you wonder if you can get away with jeans and a casual shirt. But what if someone you want to impress walks in off the street? Maybe you should dress nicely just in case.

Bus or car? If you take the bus you'll finally have a chance to read that report. If you drive you'll get to the office quicker, but parking is always a pain in the butt. Still, who wants to be waiting around at a bus stop in the cold? You decide to drive.

Studies have shown that humans have a limited capacity for decision making over the course of a given day. Every decision, no matter how big or small, drains our energy.

The more decisions we have to make, the less capable we are of making the next decision a good one.

Which is why by the end of the day we resort to:

- Taking the easiest option available to us. ("I'll stay here at the office rather than going to the gym.")
- Maintaining the status quo. ("I can't decide between the two applicants for this role so I'll hold off on hiring anyone for now.")
- Making no decision at all. ("It's too hard to decide which of these new logos I like the most. I'll decide tomorrow when I'm less tired.")

If you're running a business, you know that being able to make good decisions at any time of the day is crucial to your success. So what can you do to ensure there are always good reserves of that precious energy on hand?

1. Have routines

Get up at the same time every morning. Have the same thing for breakfast. Wear the same thing to work each day.

Hopefully Shortcut 11 sold you on that fact that routines significantly reduce cognitive load by reducing how much you have to think about a particular task. Anything you do every single day should have a routine built around it.

2. Build good habits by making certain things non-negotiable

With things like exercise, it's been shown that exercising every day is an easier habit to maintain than exercising three days a week. Why? because there's no decision to make about which days you'll exercise. You just do it every day.

A habit has the same effect as a routine—it reduces your cognitive load. It's useful to build good habits around things that usually require willpower—exercise, eating well, meditation, reading, journaling, making sales calls, tracking statistics, etc.

3. Use a calendar instead of a to-do list

As a rule, when we sit down at the start of a day we have a list of things we need to get done. We spend a lot of energy deciding which to-do we should do first. We also tend to do the easier jobs first. And by the end of the day, making a decision to do the harder jobs requires willpower we no longer have.

So don't use a to-do list.

Using a calendar, schedule in the exact time slot you'll do each item on your to-do list. It will help with decision fatigue and getting things done, and quite possibly show you how unrealistic your to-do list is.

Summing up

Stop negotiating with yourself from the moment you wake up. By establishing sound morning routines, good daily habits and solid workday scheduling, you'll remove most of the unnecessary decision making from your day. And when you have to make a big decision, you'll have the energy you need to make the right one.

SHORTCUT 20: GET COMFORTABLE BEING UNCOMFORTABLE

It's a very rare business situation where you work hard for x number of years, get things to a certain point, and then sit on a beach in the Bahamas watching the money roll in. I won't say it never happens, but it's rare enough that it's unlikely to happen to you. (Sorry.)

What I've discovered for myself (and noticed in others) is that no matter how successful you are, having your own business is always going to involve some level of discomfort:

- The product you've been living large off for ten years might suddenly become irrelevant. (Digital cameras, anyone?)
- Financial markets can collapse.
- Booms will come to an end.
- Bubbles will burst.

Twice now my husband and I have experienced incidents (one sudden and one gradual) that wiped out cash reserves we'd spent years building up in our businesses. It was heartbreaking to see those cash reserves decimated. But you might also argue it was the reason we built up cash reserves in the first place.

Here's what those experiences taught me:

- Never take the good times for granted.
- Always use those good times to put money away for the bad.
- Some things in business (and life) are very much out of your control.
- If you have great emotional resilience, you can face down any challenge life throws at you and come out the other side thriving.

This is what I find most exciting about being a business owner—it's never boring because things are constantly evolving. And we're forced to evolve both ourselves and our businesses to keep up.

Which is why I think one of the most important 'shortcuts' to business success is getting comfortable with knowing that being a business owner will always involve a level of discomfort.

I know that once I wrapped my head around this idea, I started to enjoy the perks of the 'job' a lot more—the extra flexibility, the earning power, and the unparalleled ability to be the master of my own destiny.

WHERE TO FROM HERE?

Hey, hey! You've gotten to the end of the book. I'm thrilled. I know I struggle to get to the end of most business books I read these days,

Since you're here, it's important to now take the time to consider this question:

What should I do now?

So often we listen to podcasts or read books and nod along thinking "Hey, yeah! I can do that", or "I should do that". But then we close the book or put our headphones away and forget all about that great thing we could do.

I hate the thought of providing inspiration that doesn't lead to action so please take some time now to choose just one shortcut from this book to put into action over the next month. Given every single one of the shortcuts has been road-tested by me in the real world, I guarantee it doesn't matter which one you choose, it will have a positive effect on your business.

If you're looking for accountability, I can help with that too!

Just email **kelly@kellyexeter.com.au** and tell me which thing you're going to do. I promise to follow up with you in a month to see how you went!

You can also go to **swishdesign.com.au/accountable** to join the list for daily '10-minute-a-day' marketing prompts. I really believe that, more than anything, making a 10-minute daily commitment to market your business will be something you look back on in a year's time and think 'That was what made all the difference to my business'.

A SPECIAL REQUEST FROM ME

As an independent author, I am completely reliant on my readers and my personal network to spread the word about my books. If you found this book useful, I'd love you to write a 2-3 line review on Amazon and/or Goodreads sharing:

- Which bit particularly resonated with you
- What kind of person you think this book will help.

If you do write a review somewhere, please let me know via email (**kelly@kellyexeter.com.au**) so I can personally thank you :)

ACKNOWLEDGEMENTS

This book was born out of a challenge Meryl Johnston threw down to a Mastermind group I belong to: **#writeeverydayinmay**. At that time, since I already wrote every day, I made my challenge a little tougher. I decided I'd write one quality blog post for the Swish Design site on every working day that May. It nearly killed me. But what doesn't kill you makes you stronger, RIGHT?! And from those words, this book emerged. So, thank you Meryl!

Thanks also to James Schramko for being able to share his profit formula twice in this book. James was at pains to emphasise it's not 'his' formula as it's the adaptation of a few things he's come across out there. But James is the one who introduced me to the formula so as far as I'm concerned, it's his!

To Bill Harper and Kym Campradt—my editing/proofing dream team. I'm often told that my books make for 'easy reading' and a lot of that is Bill's ability to simultaneously sharpen and simplify sentences. Kym's keen proofreading eyes pick up all the dodgy stuff I do to Bill's sharpening once a manuscript is back in my hands.

To our clients at Swish Design—really, I wrote this book for you. If it helps you run your business more profitably and/or achieve a better quality of life while running your business, then my job here is done!

And finally, to Ant. As I said in the dedication of this book, most of the stuff in here are the shortcuts you tried to give me over the years. As always, however, I had to learn the hard way. But hey, I got there in the end :)

Printed in Poland
by Amazon Fulfillment
Poland Sp. z o.o., Wrocław